ALTERNATOR BOOKS™

SPACE IN ACTION

SPACE VEHICLES IN ACTION

An AUGMENTED REALITY Experience

Rebecca E. Hirsch

T0018669

Lerner Publications ◆ Minneapolis

EXPLORE SPACE IN BRAND-NEW WAYS WITH AUGMENTED REALITY!

1. Ask a parent or guardian for permission to download the free Lerner AR app on your digital device by going to the App Store or Google Play.

2. As you read, look for this icon throughout the book. It means there is an augmented reality experience on that page!

3. Use the Lerner AR app to scan the picture near the icon.

4. Watch space come alive with augmented reality!

CONTENTS

INTRODUCTION
ROCKET MAN   4

CHAPTER 1
ROCKETS   6

CHAPTER 2
SATELLITES   14

CHAPTER 3
LANDERS   20

CHAPTER 4
DEEP SPACE VEHICLES   24

3D PRINTER MODELS   28

GLOSSARY   29

FURTHER INFORMATION   30

INDEX   31

INTRODUCTION
ROCKET MAN

Launch day was here. A giant rocket called Falcon Heavy sat on a launchpad in Florida on February 6, 2018. The rocket held surprising cargo: a bright red sports car with a dummy in the front seat. The car and dummy helped draw attention to the launch.

Falcon Heavy was the world's most powerful active rocket when it launched in 2018.

SPACEX

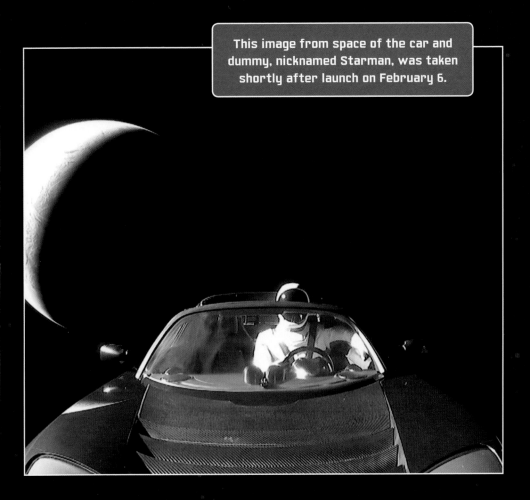

This image from space of the car and dummy, nicknamed Starman, was taken shortly after launch on February 6.

Falcon Heavy, built by the US company SpaceX, was a new, powerful rocket. This launch was a test. Someday Falcon Heavy might carry people deep into space.

Finally, the moment came. Liftoff! The rocket arced a fiery path in the sky. The crowd cheered as Falcon Heavy disappeared from view into the blackness of space.

CHAPTER 1

ROCKETS

Imagine traveling through deep space on a journey that could take a year or more. The farthest people have gone from Earth is the moon, but that may soon change. The next generation of rockets might carry astronauts to Mars and other distant parts of the **solar system**.

Astronaut Charles M. Duke Jr. walks on the moon in 1972. Twelve astronauts have visited the lunar surface.

Rockets are vehicles that launch astronauts and cargo into space. Rocket engines use a force called **thrust**. You can watch thrust in action if you let go of an untied, inflated balloon. The escaping air creates thrust, and the balloon goes flying in the opposite direction. A rocket engine burns fuel and sends hot gas through an opening at its bottom. The force of the escaping gas pushes the rocket off the ground. Blastoff!

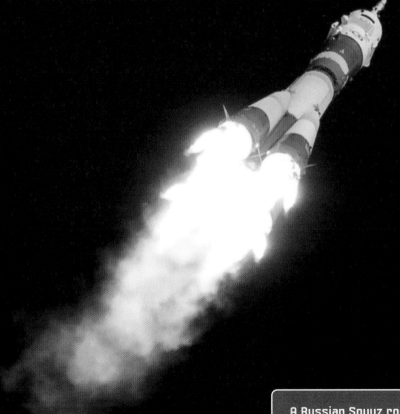

A Russian Soyuz rocket launches in 2017.

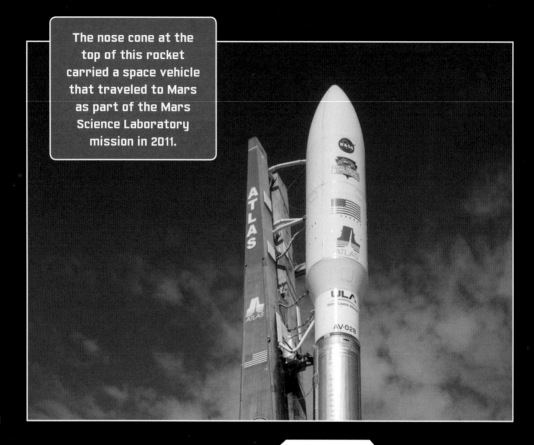

The nose cone at the top of this rocket carried a space vehicle that traveled to Mars as part of the Mars Science Laboratory mission in 2011.

Modern rockets are often made of two or three connected rockets. Each rocket is a **stage**. The first stage carries the entire spacecraft into the sky. When the first stage runs out of fuel, it disconnects and falls to Earth. The second stage takes over before it too runs out of fuel and falls away. The final stage has a nose cone that carries a space vehicle, such as a **satellite** or capsule. When the final stage reaches space, its nose cone opens. The space vehicle continues the journey as the final stage falls away.

ROCKET POWER

When Falcon Heavy launched on its test flight in 2018, it was the biggest, most powerful rocket in use in the world. It stood 230 feet (70 m) tall, as high as a twenty-three-story building. It could launch as much **mass** as five school buses into Earth's **orbit**.

The two rockets on the sides of Falcon Heavy are boosters. The boosters help lift the main rocket and are designed to fall away and land on Earth.

The most powerful rocket in history was the Saturn V. It stood 363 feet (111 m) tall, higher than the Statue of Liberty. It could launch mass equal to ten school buses into orbit.

Full of fuel at launch, a Saturn V rocket weighed 6.2 million pounds (2.8 million kg).

Saturn V rockets launched Apollo mission flights between 1967 and 1972. These included Apollo 11, the mission that landed the first people on the moon. The last Saturn V journey, in 1973, launched an entire **space station**, Skylab, into Earth's orbit.

NASA is working on the most powerful rocket ever built. Space Launch System will stand 321 feet (98 m) tall, about as high as a thirty-story building. It will be able to carry incredible amounts of cargo into space, as well as space capsules.

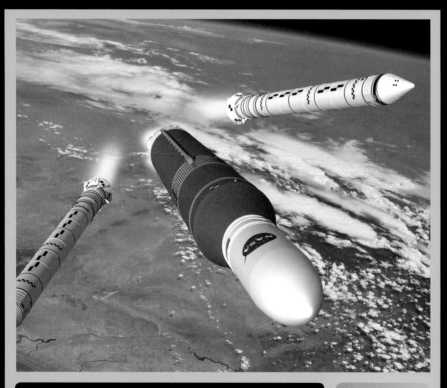

The first Space Launch System will carry only cargo, but later versions of the rocket will bring astronauts to space.

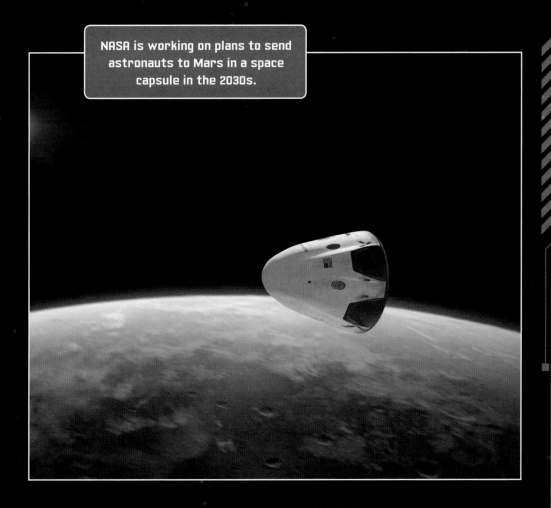

NASA is working on plans to send astronauts to Mars in a space capsule in the 2030s.

A space capsule has everything people need to survive, such as air, water, and food. The vehicle is also designed to return astronauts safely to Earth. A giant rocket may someday carry a capsule into space as the first step on a journey to an asteroid or Mars.

SATELLITES

In October 1957, the first vehicle made by humans reached space. *Sputnik* looked like a silver beach ball with four antennae. Launched by the former Soviet Union, a group of fifteen republics including Russia, *Sputnik* orbited Earth for three months. Then it fell and burned up in Earth's **atmosphere**.

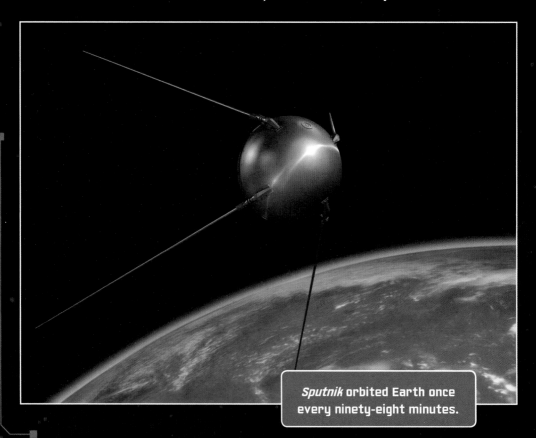

Sputnik orbited Earth once every ninety-eight minutes.

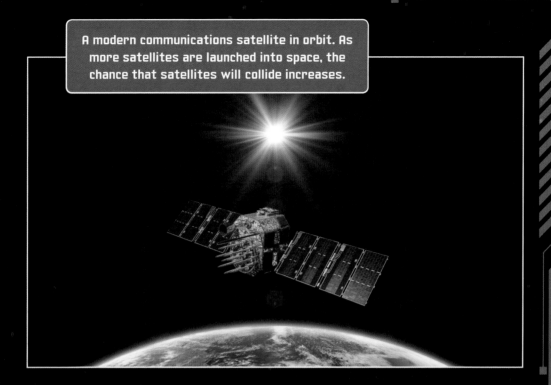

A modern communications satellite in orbit. As more satellites are launched into space, the chance that satellites will collide increases.

Satellites orbit Earth or another object in space. A satellite stays in orbit because its speed balances the pull of the object's gravity. If the satellite moves too fast, it flies off into space. Too slow, and it falls to the surface of the planet or moon.

IN EARTH'S ORBIT

In the twenty-first century, thousands of satellites orbit Earth, and they sometimes collide. In 2009 a Russian satellite and a US satellite crashed into each other. Space organizations keep track of satellite positions and try to prevent collisions, but sometimes they are impossible to avoid.

Scientists use satellites to study our oceans, land, and atmosphere. **Meteorologists** use them to track storms and predict the weather. Communications satellites relay phone calls or radio signals. The signals go to a satellite in orbit. Then the satellite sends them to different locations on the ground.

A satellite image shows Hurricane Gonzalo (*lower right*) near the east coast of the United States in 2017.

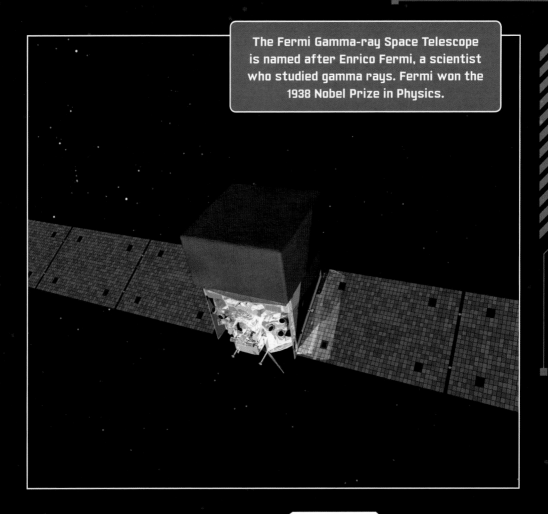

The Fermi Gamma-ray Space Telescope is named after Enrico Fermi, a scientist who studied gamma rays. Fermi won the 1938 Nobel Prize in Physics.

Other Earth-orbiting satellites face outward, into space. They may watch for dangerous particles coming from the sun or help us study the universe. NASA's Fermi Gamma-ray Space Telescope studies gamma rays, a powerful kind of light that we can't see. Gamma rays help us learn about parts of the universe that are hard to study, such as black holes and exploding stars.

ORBITING OTHER WORLDS

Many satellites orbit moons or other planets. NASA's *Odyssey* has been orbiting Mars since 2001. With high-powered cameras, *Odyssey* searches for evidence of water and ice on the Red Planet. It monitors weather conditions, including dust storms.

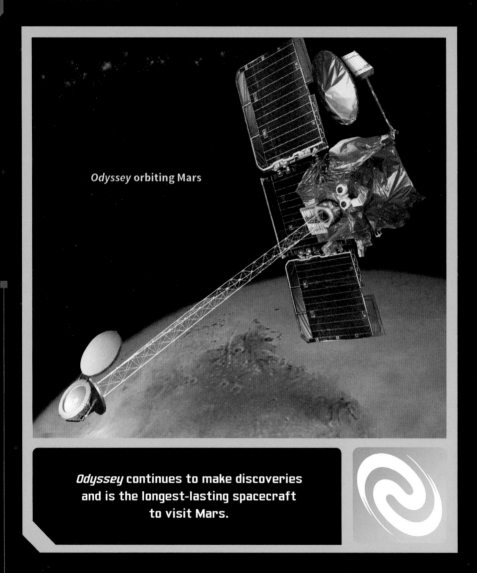

Odyssey orbiting Mars

Odyssey continues to make discoveries and is the longest-lasting spacecraft to visit Mars.

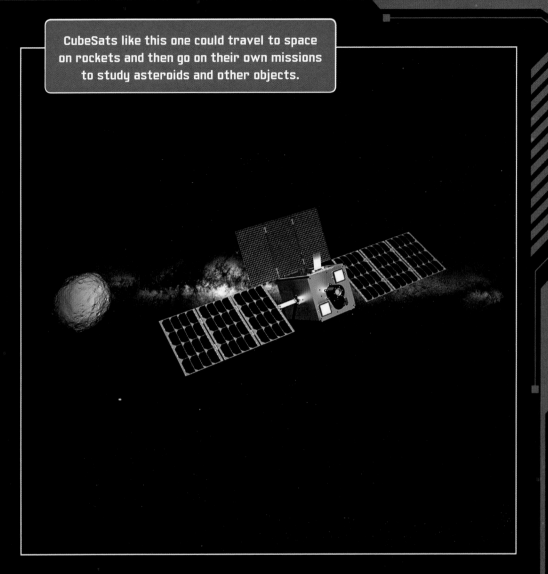

CubeSats like this one could travel to space on rockets and then go on their own missions to study asteroids and other objects.

Satellites can be large. *Cassini*, a satellite that orbited Saturn from 2004 to 2017, was about as big as a school bus. But satellites don't have to be big. Modern miniature satellites, called CubeSats, are about the size of a briefcase or even smaller.

CHAPTER 3

LANDERS

On May 5, 2018, NASA's InSight mission blasted off. Tucked inside the nose of the rocket was a lander. This robotic vehicle lands on the surface of an object in space. The *InSight* lander was headed to Mars. Scientists and engineers had programmed it with landing commands. Once *InSight* reached Mars, it was on its own to carry out the wild and tricky landing.

A rocket carries *InSight* to space from Vandenberg Air Force Base in California.

NASA technicians work on *InSight* in 2015 in full body coverings to avoid getting dust or other particles on the lander's parts.

On November 26, *InSight* reached the Martian atmosphere. It opened its parachute. The lander slowed, and its radar system locked onto the ground to determine its exact position above Mars. *InSight* let go of its parachute and fired miniature rocket engines to slow its descent.

Two CubeSats had ridden along on the InSight mission, and they were in orbit above Mars. The tiny satellites beamed signals back to Earth during the landing. They allowed people in mission control to monitor the landing almost in real time. When the lander touched down on Mars, everyone cheered. *InSight* had nailed the landing!

LANDER HOT SPOTS

Landers have visited Earth's moon. They have visited Venus, Mars, and Mercury, as well as Saturn's moon, Titan. In 2018 landers from the United States and Japan arrived on asteroids. Their goal is to collect samples of dust and rocks and send them back to Earth. Japan's mission will return the samples to Earth in 2020, and the US mission will return in 2023.

NASA's *OSIRIS-REx* lander arrived at asteroid Bennu in December 2018.

This artist's impression shows a lander surrounded by airbags after touching down on the surface of Mars.

Mars has been a hot spot for landings. *InSight* was the eighth successful landing there. In 1976 *Viking 1* and *Viking 2* became the first spacecraft to land on Mars. Like *InSight*, these landers used small rockets to slow their descent.

Other Mars landers used airbags. The airbags inflated seconds before touchdown. The landers bounced and rolled across the ground. When they came to a stop, the airbags deflated.

CHAPTER 4

DEEP SPACE VEHICLES

On November 5, 2018, *Voyager 2*, a robotic vehicle, left the solar system. It was 11 billion miles (17.7 billion km) from the sun. *Voyager 2* had left the **heliosphere**, a giant bubble of **charged particles** created by the sun. The outer edge of the heliosphere marks the outer limits of the solar system. *Voyager 2* was the second vehicle to leave the heliosphere. The first was its twin, *Voyager 1*. It left the solar system in 2012.

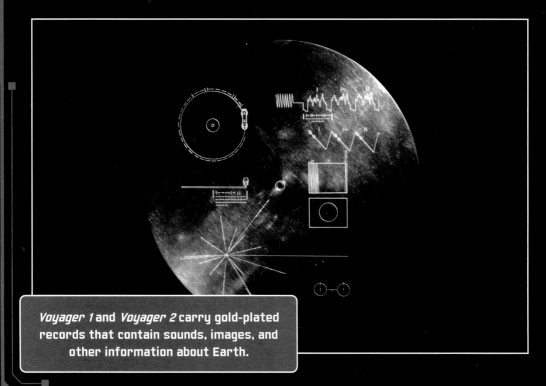

Voyager 1 and *Voyager 2* carry gold-plated records that contain sounds, images, and other information about Earth.

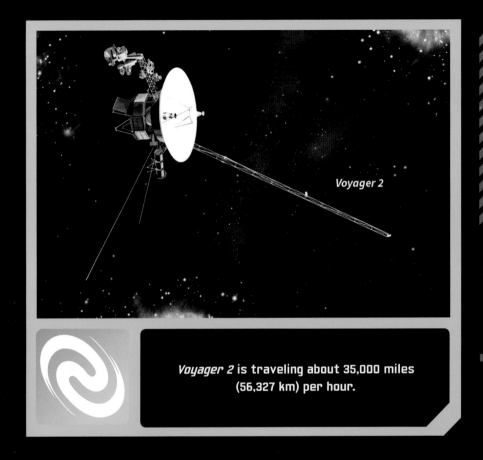

Voyager 2

Voyager 2 is traveling about 35,000 miles (56,327 km) per hour.

NASA launched *Voyager 1* and *Voyager 2* in 1977. The Voyager missions are the longest-running space missions in history. Between them, the vehicles visited Jupiter, Saturn, Uranus, and Neptune.

Scientists expect the spacecraft to keep communicating with Earth until at least 2025. Sometime later, the fuel that powers their instruments will run out and they will continue speeding through space in silence. The probes each carry a gold record to provide information about Earth to alien life that might find the vehicles. The record carries pictures and sounds from Earth, and includes spoken greetings in fifty-five languages.

INTO THE FUTURE

Newer space vehicles are also sailing through distant parts of the solar system. *New Horizons* is exploring the Kuiper Belt, a band of rocks and ice beyond Neptune. *New Horizons* has taken close-up images of the most distant objects ever explored.

Scientists and engineers are designing new space capsules that will carry astronauts to distant parts of the solar system. Orion is a new spacecraft from NASA that will carry up to four astronauts deeper into space than ever before. Then it will return them safely to Earth.

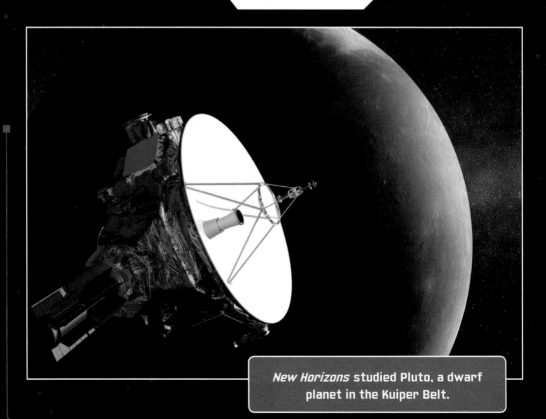

New Horizons studied Pluto, a dwarf planet in the Kuiper Belt.

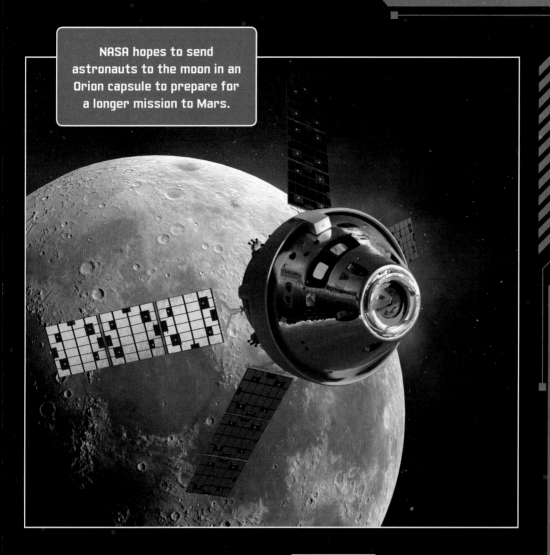

NASA hopes to send astronauts to the moon in an Orion capsule to prepare for a longer mission to Mars.

In 2014 NASA sent Orion on a successful test flight with a powerful rocket. When the Space Launch System is finished, NASA will test it for carrying Orion and cargo into space. If all goes well, astronauts may travel aboard Orion to a distant asteroid, Mars, or even beyond.

Follow the links below to download 3D printer design files for some of the vehicles in this book:

Odyssey, http://qrs.lernerbooks.com/MarsOdyssey

Orion, http://qrs.lernerbooks.com/Orion

Space Launch System, http://qrs.lernerbooks.com/SLS

Viking Lander, http://qrs.lernerbooks.com/Viking

Voyager 1, http://qrs.lernerbooks.com/Voyager

atmosphere: a mass of gases surrounding a planet

charged particles: pieces of matter smaller than atoms that carry an electric charge

heliosphere: a region of space containing charged particles created by the sun. The heliosphere surrounds the sun and planets.

mass: the amount of matter in an object

meteorologists: scientists who study the atmosphere and predict the weather

orbit: the path around a body in space, or to move along that path

satellite: a vehicle that travels in orbit around a planet, moon, or other body in space

solar system: a star and all the planets, moons, and objects that orbit it

space station: a large spacecraft that orbits Earth and is occupied by people for long periods

stage: one of the sections of a rocket having its own fuel and engine

thrust: a forward or upward force produced by a rocket engine

FURTHER INFORMATION

Dlugos, Jenn. *Stellar Space Technology and Exploration: 40 Amazing Infographics for Kids*. Waco, TX: Prufrock, 2019.

Ives, Rob. *Build Your Own Rockets and Planes*. Minneapolis: Hungry Tomato, 2018.

Kenney, Karen Latchana. *Cutting-Edge Journey to Mars*. Minneapolis: Lerner Publications, 2020.

Mara, Wil. *Breakthroughs in Space Travel*. Minneapolis: Lerner Publications, 2019.

NASA Kids' Club
https://www.nasa.gov/kidsclub/index.html

NASA Space Place: Build a Bubble-Powered Rocket!
https://spaceplace.nasa.gov/pop-rocket/en/

StarChild: Space Travel
https://starchild.gsfc.nasa.gov/docs/StarChild/space_level2/travel.html

What Was the Apollo Program?
https://www.nasa.gov/audience/forstudents/5-8/features/nasa-knows/what-was-apollo-program-58.html

INDEX

Cassini, 19

Falcon Heavy, 4–5, 9
Fermi Gamma-ray Space
    Telescope, 17

InSight, 20–21, 23

Jupiter, 25

Kuiper Belt, 26

Mars, 6, 13, 18, 20–23, 27
Mercury, 22

NASA, 12, 17–18, 20, 25–27
Neptune, 25–26
New Horizons, 26

Odyssey, 18

Saturn, 19, 22, 25
Saturn V, 10–11
SpaceX, 5
Sputnik, 14

Uranus, 25

Venus, 22
Viking 1, 23
Viking 2, 23
Voyager 1, 24–25
Voyager 2, 24–25

Photo Acknowledgments

Image credits: Freer/Shutterstock.com, p. 2 (bottom); courtesy of SpaceX, pp. 4, 5, 9, 13; NASA, pp. 6, 10, 11, 12, 17, 24; NASA/Joel Kowsky, p. 7; NASA/Scott Andrews, p. 8; EduardHarkonen/Getty Images, p. 14; BlackJack3D/Getty Images, p. 15; NOAA/NASA GOES Project, p. 16; NASA/JPL, pp. 18, 25; ESA/Jacky Huart, p. 19; NASA/Ben Smegelsky, p. 20; NASA/JPL/Caltech/Lockheed Martin, p. 21; NASA Goddard Space Flight Center, p. 22; NASA/JPL/Caltech, p. 23; NASA/Johns Hopkins University Applied Physics Laboratory/Southwest Research Institute, p. 26; Lockheed Martin Corporation, p. 27. Design elements: Jetrel/Shutterstock.com; Nanashiro/Shutterstock.com; phiseksit/Shutterstock.com; MSSA/Shutterstock.com; Pakpoom Makpan/Shutterstock.com; pixelparticle/Shutterstock.com; wacomka/Shutterstock.com; fluidworkshop/Shutterstock.com.

Cover: NASA/JPL-Caltech.

Lerner Publications Company
An imprint of Lerner Publishing Group, Inc.
241 First Avenue North
Minneapolis, MN 55401 USA

For reading levels and more information, look up this title at www.lernerbooks.com.

Main body text set in Aptifer Sans LT Pro.
Typeface provided by Linotype AG.

Library of Congress Cataloging-in-Publication Data

Names: Hirsch, Rebecca E., author.
Title: Space vehicles in action : an augmented reality experience / Rebecca E. Hirsch.
Description: Minneapolis : Lerner Publications, [2020] | Series: Space in action
    (Alternator books) | Audience: Ages 8–12. | Audience: Grades 4 to 6. | Includes
    bibliographical references and index.
Identifiers: LCCN 2019013121 (print) | LCCN 2019013931 (ebook) |
    ISBN 9781541583528 (eb pdf) | ISBN 9781541578821 (lb : alk. paper)
Subjects: LCSH: Space vehicles—Juvenile literature. | Artificial satellites—Juvenile
    literature. | Outer space—Exploration—Juvenile literature.
Classification: LCC TL795 (ebook) | LCC TL795 .H57 2020 (print) | DDC 629.44—dc23

LC record available at https://lccn.loc.gov/2019013121

Manufactured in the United States of America
1-46985-47854-7/10/2019